Seventy Times Seven

by Hyacinthe L. Raven

Via Dolorosa Press
Cleveland, Ohio

Seventy Times Seven

© 2013 by Hyacinthe L. Raven

Cover art by Elisabeth Butler

Title font "The King and Queen" by bran
(www.imbran.net)

Title and quote taken from "Dolores (Notre-Dame des Sept Douleurs)" by Algernon Charles Swinburne from *Swinburne's Collected Poetical Works*, 2 vols. (London: William Heinemann, 1924): I, 154-68.

vdp55

Library of Congress Control Number: 2013947976
ISBN-10: 0-9718673-8-0
ISBN-13: 978-0-9718673-8-3

Via Dolorosa Press
701 East Schaaf Road
Cleveland, OH 44131
USA
www.viadolorosapress.com

To

Mara Morrigan

&

Antoinette Hancock,

my anchors in this storm

She slays, and her hands are not bloody;

She moves as a moon in the wane,

White-robed, and thy raiment is ruddy,

Our Lady of Pain.

-A. C. Swinburne

1

This is how the moment begins:
Me, waist-deep in torment,
Dolores covered in snow.
It's not enough that
I am still open-armed.
Sometimes things have to be
that way.
Sometimes the sky does not care,
and your feet plant themselves
deep in the earth.

2

It was a long
winter, one
that settled
scores and left
little ink
to write with.

Dolores was not
oblivious to this,
had not forgotten
what brought
us to this point,

together.

3

Across the pond
we met, a year
or a lifetime

earlier, drawn
to the other
by verses caught
in the ether.
Poets both:
one classic, one
not; one
laud, one lorn;

each longing
completion.

4

Those lost months
were almost too
long to wait for
her to come to me.

We made do with
the rare voice
over crackling lines,
or the perfume
of ink on paper,

writing our story
to web over the
ocean, yearning
to draw our
juicy prey
within ourselves.

5

To say I was caught
in a spell would be an
understatement; I
loved Dolores, the
dried rose beauty
of her. I
needed Dolores, the
texture of layers
upon layers of wisdom.

Those dark eyes,
those pursed lips...

I did as I was told,
mirrored in her sight
and held in a glass
box between her fingers.

6

We shared more
unspoken than
not. Words were
always only barbs

or balm, nothing
more, despite our
art. Speech was

better through
touch, our lips
or hands spelling
out what could
never be translated

in any language
we uttered. Like
braille, but deeper,

fathomless,

intrinsic.

7

Dolores was a
monument,
carved of
alabaster but
pulsing thick
red within,

staked deep
in the soft
muscle of
my heart

like a papercut
from a love letter,
the sharp prick
from a rose thorn,

or the bright singe
from that first touch.

8

Vignettes, she
murmurs against
the hollow of
my throat, a
smile warming
the blood in
her lips. *You*

*write such telling
vignettes.* Her
teeth pull at my
skin, a dull
pain. *Dark
scenes, such
shadow in
your big hazel*

eyes. My breath
rustles her soft
strands of black
silk, gasping, and

I can say nothing.

9

Dolores is exquisite
in the moonlight,

especially in this
cold, icy winter.
Her pale skin
glitters beneath
me, captured in
the tears that
well at the
corners of my
eyes. She likes

to whisper poems
to me while
I make love
to her. What her
voice says, my lips
reenact on her
flesh. The taste

of her is spicy
incense, with a
tinge of something
that says she's
been around

far beyond
her years.
My fingertips
smooth her long
black hair from
her forehead, tracing
down her face
to paint in the
lusty sheen on

her skin, the
veil I place
each night on
my ancient bride.

10

She's had about
enough of this already,
looking out the window
at the changing weather.
The blood's too thick
this far north, the
spirit not as free.

There is a special place
out there for us,
the alpha and omega,
a place where the
womb and tomb meet,
shrouded in all
we hold dear.

This Dolores swore,
and I believed her
like an eager child
grasping at a
stranger's candy.

11

If you look deep into
Dolores's stone eyes,

beneath the
layer of ice,

hidden at the
center of the
crystal,

you can see the
beginnings of hope.

12

There was something
Dolores wanted to
tell me, but she

kept skirting the
issue, like the
snowflakes that
tempted my lips
only to pull
back at the last
moment. Her

eyes betrayed
her silence;
it was
something

I would not
want to hear.

13

Don't write
tonight,
my love.

Give the ink
time to dry,
the thought
time to cure.

Clutched
tightly to
her breast,
Dolores
begged me,
worshipped me,

owned me
with her
fateful kiss.

14

She talked me into
moving south.

I should have known
from the start that
it was rash,
but there really
was no arguing;

what Dolores wanted,
Dolores got.

I bade farewell
to my beloved city,
the one Dolores
called The Mistake
On The Lake, her
lips roped into
a sly smirk

like a tiny
triumph over
nature.

Spring's aroma
of rotting fish
had dissipated,
but the mossy
green of the
water did not.

I gazed teary-eyed
at its murky
stillness and imagined
the first time I
swallowed Erie's
heady flavor,

a cruel trick
of a sudden tide.
It was a potion
that would either
kill me or make
me invincible.
Her Chosen One,
it was the latter.

Cleveland runs deep
in my veins. I
will go where Dolores
asks, but home
I take with me.

16

Dolores wants me to
do that trick I
do with my lips.

She has whispered
this to me no less
than four times now.

We are enroute
to Chicago, rocking
gently together with
the sway of the
train, her breasts
pressed softly against
mine like skeins
of yarn in a
knitter's basket.

We are not alone
enough for me to
do what she asks,

despite the dimmed
lights and snoring.

There are bodies

set around us,
various-hued dominoes
that could topple
at the impending sound
emanating deep within her.

Dolores is not pleased.

17

It's like a palace,
she says, staring
at the endless ceiling.
Or a cathedral.

Yes, a cathedral,
its pews filled with
people who don't
realize that they
shouldn't be talking.
Not now, not yet.

Dolores wants to
leave an offering.
We've nothing,
but this is now
my quest, she
begs me with
a kiss. A sacrifice

for our journey.
Union Station looks
lovely on her,
perched as she is
on a wooden bench,
sunlight cascading

over her dark hair,
praying and praying.

18

We are heading in
the wrong direction.

The train jolts
out, softening only
after I see that we
are not moving
south. Dolores's

prayers told her
that this was the
way. Out west
there is something
we must claim first;

the ocean, we
haven't touched
the ocean together,
or the stars, how
clear they will
be, clearer than
we've ever seen.

She is so beautiful
like this, eyes
glimmering with hope

and reverance.

My heart dies
a bit, the second
time in as many
days. An omen
or love, I know
not which. Only
that my fingers
touch silver when
they touch her face.

A dead horse, slumped
into a pile like an
old army tent
collapsed onto its poles.

Dolores saw this,
swore it was
there on the
plains, the
shadow next
to a rusty
tractor, alone in
its open grave.

She's shivering
now, huddled
against me as
the train continues
on, unapologetic.
Her eyes have not
moved from the
smudged glass, as
if turning away
were the foulest
insult one could
give to that poor

animal, the way
it is when a
street beggar's
gaze is not met.

20

When Dolores
was in England,
I looked at
these same

stars, though
not as bright
as they are
here, alone,

wondering
if they told
her how long
I stared, how
hard I wished

I could just
touch her face
and tell her
I was lost
without her,

I was nothing
without her,
how I was
waiting, waiting,

always waiting.

And now, somewhere
between Chicago
and Portland, with
no place to go
but within, I
cannot tell
her anything.

She awoke in
my arms as the
rugged mountains
came into view,
wisps of sunlight
glittering the slight
moisture between
her lashes. Against

such a backdrop,
I worshipped the
soft curve of her
eyelids and held her
venerably, as if
she had just died.

No, just the silence,
my beautiful Dolores;

please let me
have just one
moment more.

22

Portland weeps
even when the
sun is out.

It's a feeling we
don't have back
in Cleveland, that
lush mist in the
air, holographic
rainbow in the sky.
We have only grey,

monochrome and
no words, because

there are none
left to say.

Here, they are
overwhelmed,
full on it,
too much beauty
to be held
aloft. It has to
seep out some-
where; there

is no choice.

So, we stretch
our arms out
to those tears,
catching them
on hands and faces,

lips and tongues,

until our skin
is sated, effulgent.

23

Today, we are
children. We are
secret loves in
long cotton dressing
gowns, stealing away
enchanted moments
in a damp forest.

The train is behind
us now, and the
buildings here
are solid hints
of fairy tales.
We duck behind
resin mushroom
houses and pretend
this is where we
belong. I've never
seen such a place.

Dolores tells me a
man created it
for his little
ones, and now
we are them. She

tastes like candy
floss and will not
stop twirling.

*This is what we
were meant to find,*

she says, feeding
me with deep kisses.
This is where her
prayers led us.

24

God wanted us
to go south now,
down the coast.

He showed us the
craggy caves filled
with the rustling
sound of sea lions,
and we couldn't help
but smile at their
freedom among
the rock and tide.

We thanked Him
later on the beach,
limbs entwined
against the wet
altar of flesh, our
own flavors now
that of the melding
sea spray and salt.

The stars in Dolores's
eyes were the
stars in the clear
night sky, so much

His that my heart

died again
when she came.

25

They stretch to heaven,
like musty elevators.
They block out the sun,
letting us flit in and
around fallen branches,
dryads hiding just as
easily in the day as
we would at night.

I love these trees,
could carve our
home out of them,
endless real estate.

For a moment, I think
Dolores enjoys what this
feeling looks like on me.

For a moment, it is no
longer me against God.

The wanderlust
is wearing thin.

Dolores needs
to be settled now,

but we are still
too far away.

This was her
idea, so it cannot
be wrong. And

this was the
first sign that
there lay a
chasm somewhere
beneath the love
and lust. But
for now, my

apology, instead,
will suffice.

Dolores is manic
and on a mission.
Somehow, we must
reach Pier 39, not
passing Go, not
collecting $200, so
that we can capture
a delicacy so elusive
only she knows of it.

Great pains we must
take in this pursuit.
We cannot see the
city or people, the
bay or bridge, even
though she knows
I've never been
here, nor this far.

When she finally
fills my hands with
the hot little rings
of dough, I laugh.

We had these at
home, of course, but

she never
even noticed.

28

It's time to head east
now; Dolores is done
with California. My

response to San
Francisco's treasure
was not what she
had in mind, and
the sting of her
five-pointed hand
changed our direction,

like a sudden storm
over old Erie.

When I finally
open my eyes,
I think she has
left me. There is
nothing but light,
bright, glaring light.

But this is no
dream. It is Vegas,
loud as an oasis,

the showiest of
all my prisons.

30

Dolores has not let
me out of her sight,
not for a second.

Even when my eyes
close again and I
think I am forsaken,
she is there. When
she locks the door
behind us, she hides
the key and claims
me roughly like a
man, a frustrated
Priapus with some-
thing to prove.

She does not stop
until she can taste
my tears, until her
nails have scraped
my insides raw
with her power.

Something changed
in those moments
last night. Was

it resentment
that coated her
tongue? Did
my prone body

betray my thoughts,
scare the longing
out of her? She

is not nursing
my wounds
today. She

is, instead,
tearing pages
from my diary,

shamed by
my devotion.

Static from the t.v.
crackles between
Dolores's shallow, stifled
breaths, the sheets
trapping the stale air
she breathes as I watch
her from another bed.

It's strange how
people follow dreams,
think they might
understand,
think they might
have finally fallen
in love. And

strange how
it never feels
as good as
it should.

There is nothing
out here in
the desert.

Dolores tells me
that I haven't
looked hard enough,

that I don't
understand that
some things just

need more work,
more investment.

(The mirror she
holds has no
reflection.)

.

34

She hated me
at that moment,
when she didn't
see tears welling
in my eyes. How

could I not
be moved by
this feat of
nature, this
impossible
beauty? Oh,

but I was.
No apathy, just
concentration,
(l'appel du vide)
memorization,

assessing every crevice,
every edge, imagining
the soft, wet sound of
contact, calculating the
exact point where one
would lose sight and
assume that it was

a bird, loose rock,
a wave of heat in
this grand mirage.
Oh yes, it was a
beautiful place, an
inspirational place.

It was her,
what she meant
to me, in all
her scorching
glory,

that first
instance when
I tasted it,

the bitter
tang of
death.

35

Almost to the
Promised Land,

we were strangers.
The changing
scenery like
four countries
in two hours,

nomads,

hoping to outrun
the fading sun.

Dolores is going
to be a professor,

this she
professes
as we cross
the border into
Louisiana, the

rain dropping
slowly, lightly,
punctuating
each word.

I want to
laugh, with
joy and spite,
seeing the warm
blush of intent
on her cheeks,

the way she
grips the steering
wheel as we
drive deeper into
the grey sky.

Swinburne
wouldn't have
known what
to do with this.

Not with the
way Dolores
was wringing
her hands,
pacing back
and forth like
an angry child.
I wanted to
shove her to
the bed, like
she would
have to me,

or grab her
shoulders
and just
shake,

til she looked
at me with
those wounded

eyes and I
could feel
nothing but
tenderness

and the hope
that one day
again we'd
stop fighting.

38

That first crack
of light across
the sky sent
Dolores straight into
my shivering arms,

her eyes glazed
over with fear,

glassine,

testing the limits
of our tentative
truce.

(It worked;
it always did.)

We made love
that night,
nervous like
virgins,
serenading
flesh the way
we did back
when the other
was just a
blank pillow
book, longing
to be written.

40

The dead dwell
above ground
here, Dolores

said with
a tinge of
anticipation.
We had arrived,

sneaking through
the city like we
were picking out
our cold plots,
each rotting building
we passed a
crypt of sorts.
Her eyes

glinted in the
peek of sunlight
we were granted
that day. This,

my dark love,
was now home.

41

When God exhaled
his first breath
on the seventh day,
Louisiana was created.

Dolores tells me this
as I unpack, sweat
drip-dripping onto
termite-eaten wood.

42

The neighbors all say
that you never get
used to the heat,
no matter how
long you stay,
and I cringe at
the possibility that
they're right.

43

Back in Cleveland,
the rain cools the
air like a Cocteau
Twins album.
But here, it leaves

you gasping,
gasping, less in
the throes of
passion
than in
the throes of
death,

strong, sweaty
hands around
the throat,

snapping, snapping,

relentless.

44

She's in the
backyard this
afternoon, planning
something romantic,
impressive, colored
in greens and reds,
pinks and purples.

I imagine a
breeze blowing,
cooling her in
this thick heat,
as I watch
from the bedroom
window. I'm
memorizing her
silhouette, the

way one shoulder
dips as she
succumbs to thought,

oblivious to the
long-tailed,
beady-eyed
rat climbing the

small palm
behind her.

45

I want to
write, but
nothing comes.

It is as
though she
has consumed
me so
entirely that

even the
words
are gone.

46

Dolores planted a
garden this year.
She says cabbage
is God's way
of showing that
He loves us.
And that is why
she refuses to plant
anything else.

When I try to water
them, she yells at
me and says we've
plenty of rain.

The leaves are all wilted.

She says God
will provide;
He doesn't need
any help.

The hurricane behind us
proves her point.

Four days later

we're still looking
for the trowel.

Dolores strokes
my hair idly,
admiring the
foggy grey
walls of the
sitting room

that we painted
today. *Like your
eyes*, I offer,
overcome by her
as I am. She
silences me with
a finger on
my creased lips,

sure as she is
that this fortress
is now wholly hers.

48

When I hear
the low rumble
of thunder, I

know she will
come again, stealing
minutes from me
within this room
she has me silently
hidden. Her kisses

are like laudanum
now, controlled and
controlling. What
was once myself

has been trans-
formed into what
she needs, what
will make her
strong, here

in this land
God has granted
her, baptized

day
after
day

in rain.

49

That last gust
tore through
the screens,

shattering what
was lately the
foyer, shards
of glass a
vision of ice,
a reminder of
home, *my home*,

while Dolores
continues to wail
behind me.

50

In the space
of ten minutes,
my fingers have
reached for
her thrice.

Dolores has
not seen it,
but knows.

She is conjuring
a cure for
the rain, for
me, for
this, in the

deep couplets
of curses.

51

Dolores tells me that
she's had enough.
The rain won't let up.
The clouds won't part,
not even for a moment.

Dolores wants out.
She's already planned
the tunnel. But a foot
into the ground you
find water. And unless
you become an island,
you're never going anywhere.

Dolores tells me that
beyond the well
there's an idea
waiting to happen.
She says she's wished
hard enough that
something's got to give.
But it's too humid
to act out the scene.
And unless you grow
a pair of wings,
you're never going anywhere.

Dolores thinks she's
got the hang of it
now.

Hair blowing in the wind
and foot tied to the
tree, she knows
how it works.
This time, she's the
island.
This time, when the sky
opens up,
the rest of the world
will float away
and she will be whole.

I want to tell her that
sometimes we are
the pier and
sometimes we are
the silt, but

she is already
marooned tonight.

53

My body is a tree,
firmly rooted in
the clay soil.

I no longer
close my eyes
when the storms
come.

I no longer
care
when the rains
drown out
the sun,
or when the
babies squeal
and cry in
open carriages.

My body
stands strong.
Not even Dolores
can make
me flinch.

Dolores wants a metal house.
She says then the boughs
won't fall into her
bedroom and the glass
won't shatter on the
kitchen table.
When the sky darkens,
she laughs,
daring God to bring it on.

Dolores doesn't listen.

It's taken me almost
three whole months
to realize this.

She speaks in odd
riddles, glorifies
herself with the macabre,
and ignores anything
touched with my voice.

This isn't death.

No, this is what
makes you pray
for it.

It's not easy
living in her
shadow. She

overwhelms me,
wearing it like
a precious
jewel around

her neck. I
am hers, I am
hers, I am
here, in this
stifling room,

listening to her
pen scrape verses
onto the pages
she tore from
my diary,

blessed blessed
Lady of Pain
and all my
joys forgotten.

57

The cats are
screeching from
the trees and
there's not much
more we can do.

Dolores tries to
lure them down
with mice,
but they can
see it's a trap.

No one gets out
of here alive.

58

*You haven't
forgotten me,
have you,* she
whispered
in the dark

through the
misplaced vents
in the wall that
connected her

bedroom to my
cobwebbed

cell. *You
haven't forgotten
what these
fingers think
of you, I hope,*

the voice rasped,
more a threat
than a wish.

No, truly,

no one gets out
of here alive.

August ought to be
a dry month,
Dolores said, scooping
water from between
the weeds.
I was back on
Rue Royal
when I tried to answer,
the humidity smothering
my words.

Dolores plucked
petals off the roses
and sighed, saying
that August ought
to be a barren month,
and that if God wouldn't
make things right,
she would.

60

I gave Dolores a
newsprint bouquet
when I returned,

after she found
her flowerbed
gazing back at her from
under three feet of water.

She grumbled that
at least the snow
waited until everything
was already dead.
And why couldn't
we just move back north?

I made a mental
note to use the
funnies next
time instead of
the obituaries,

watching Dolores
hang her head
and curse the earth.

61

Today, the sky cleared.
The first ray of light
in three weeks
melted the Perspex
and we rejoiced,
hands above our heads,
that it was
not rain.

Putting the dried
puzzle back
together.

Dolores folded
laundry as
I swept the
dirt from
the porch.

When the rain
ends, the sun
varnishes everything
it touches, and
you have to
work fast.

We lost half
the house to
the ground
around us,
but Dolores
doesn't care.
She says brown
is a color she
has learned to love.

63

Dolores came to
me tonight
with a look
in her eyes
I could not
read. We

clutched each
other desperately,

me with defeat,
she with something
else, and we

died more deaths
than I thought
possible.

64

It's too late
to start over
now. The cracks
too deep and
coming from
nowhere. Was
it California
or me? Have

I forgotten the
meaning of words
after all this
time, or did I never
even know?

65

She lured me
into the bedroom
that day and
gave me a
kitten. A

sacrifice or a
trap, I knew
not, but the
pity and fear
that tiny face
gave me as
it shivered in
my hands
made me hold

fast and vow
we'd somehow
get out.

66

There's not much
more you can give
me, you naughty

naughty girl...
her lips curled,
inhuman, a
garnet nail
slicing my thigh
open as though
it were one of
her prized swords

gleaned from the
silver collection
that hangs limply
on the jagged walls.

I am not dead.
I am something worse.

We've only enough
left for one of us.

The eternity we had
planned used too
much too quick,

and now Dolores
is running out
of options. The
screams are so
shrill I don't
know if I am
deaf or insane.

Fists and fangs,
claws and cunts,

we've burned
through it all.

Old Erie, I *am*
your Chosen One,

and I'll be damned
if I give in now.

68

She took everyone
away that she
could. (Even the
kitten, with its
trembling eyes,
was no match.)

It wasn't
all that hard
since I had

described them
so well, so
vividly, as they

were all I
had left that
wasn't her.

But the sound
of the storm,

that sound
recalled drops
against red
siding, my father,

broken-hearted
but alive, and

that was something
she couldn't have.

69

Vignettes, she
hisses against
the hollow of
my throat, a
glare boiling
the blood in
her lips. *You*

*write such telling
vignettes.* Her
teeth tear at my
skin, a sharp
pain. *A fool's
verse, beneath
me, as you*

are. The bile
is acid in my
throat, and,
seething,

I can say nothing.

When my lashes
met, the tears
came. But I
did not give in.

The storm raged
around us, more
violent than I
ever knew possible,

and the curdling
screams from
Dolores threatened
to break my
concentration. Her

fingers flailed
and grasped for me
between curses and
venom, but I held

fast, eyes closed,
begging forgiveness
from my father,
my mother, and
myself.

71

I didn't know at
that point if I was
full of strength
or feigning it,

but that's all
I had. The

rain touched
me as it touched
her, but for me
it was Erie,

thick, green,
rusty Erie,
with its poison
and its power,

reminding me
that one who
is always at
the bottom is

one who is
closest to
the anchor.

72

Dolores tried to
weave what was
left of her words

into a rope.
She threw it
towards me,
cursing then begging
for it to be
pulled. Reminding

me of how she
loved my lips half-
parted, my eyes half-
haunted, my voice
possessed of fairy
power. Oh, the

splendid seas of my
kisses, the stars,
the stars, the flurry
of flesh, *oh please,*

oh please,
dearheart...

73

I think at
that moment,

even God had

had enough.

It could have
been a split
second, or
it could have
been an eternity;

I was rooted
in the clay
beneath the silt,
watching but swaying,

as the final crack
tore through the
sky and the screams.

Dolores was there,
waiting for me,
clutching air or fire,

mouth agape.

When September arrived,
the rain washed Dolores away,

and my hands unclenched for
the first time in nine
months. The sound of
redemption taut in my
ears, sighing a breath
held since Tuesday,
until a fortnight into
the storm the ground
bore her up, matted with
weeds and sand, into the
bosom of the garden.

Sweet Dolores of the Broken Breakwall,
Sweet Dolores of the Eternal Flood,

Oh, Our Lady of Pain;

I sat with you for
half an hour, and
you never said a word.

It eventually comes
down to this:
I've a shovel and
a body and a job to do.

Dolores doesn't seem to
have anything to say
about moments such
as these.
She won't even
look at me.

It doesn't matter
to her that I
spent nearly four
hours searching for
the perfect spot.

It doesn't matter
to her that I
measured to be
sure six feet
was really six feet.
(And how impossible
a feat here in this
god-forsaken place.)

Dolores rests
against the half-dead
tree to my left.

The smirk on her face
gives me the
extra energy I need
to drag her over and
push her in.

It's what she had
always wanted,
the earth to choke
on her glory, to
be silenced with
sacrifice. Wasn't
that what she fed
me in her prayers?

Dolores was right
about one thing, at least:
God *does* work
in mysterious ways.

77

That was it.
And the drive home was tough.

But as I rattled my way
over Lake Pontchartrain,
I looked back only once:

to see the heavy storm clouds
close in over the place
where my hopes died.